CONTENTS

Pure Jazz	7
Kinds of Jazz	8
Jazz History	9
Up the River and All That Jazz	12
Ragtime	14
The Blues	17
Boogie-Woogie	19
Swing	20
New Orleans Jazz	21
Chicago Jazz	23
New York Jazz	24
Kansas City Jazz	25
Minton's	26
Into the Cool	28
Le Jazz Hot	32
British Jazz	33
Famous Names	36
Louis Armstrong	36
Count Basie	37
Sidney Bechet	37
Bix Beiderbecke	37
Buddy Bolden	38
Dave Brubeck	48
Benny Carter	38
Ornette Coleman	38
John Coltrane	39
Eddie Condon	40
Miles Davis	40
Duke Ellington	41
Bud Freeman	41
Erroll Garner	48

Dizzy Gillespie   41
Benny Goodman   42
Lionel Hampton   42
Coleman Hawkins   42
Fletcher Henderson   42
Woody Herman   43
Earl Hines   43
Billie Holiday   43
Mahalia Jackson   43
Bunk Johnson   43
James P. Johnson   44
Stan Kenton   44
John Lewis   48
Nick La Rocca   45
Red McKenzie   45
Mezz Mezzrow   45
Gerry Mulligan   45
Red Nichols   46
Charlie Parker   46
Oscar Peterson   47
Pee Wee Russell   49
Muggsy Spanier   49
Art Tatum   49
Jack Teagarden   49
Fats Waller   50
Lester Young   50
Mike Zwerin   50

How to Talk Jazz   51
  Discography   54

Glossary   58

A Question of Jazz   62

BLUFF YOUR WAY IN
JAZZ

PETER CLAYTON &
PETER GAMMOND

RAVETTE BOOKS

Published by Ravette Books Limited
3 Glenside Estate, Star Road
Partridge Green, Horsham,
West Sussex RHl3 8RA
(0403) 710392

First printed 1987
Revised 1992

Series Editor - Anne Tauté

Cover design - Jim Wire
Printing & Binding - Cox & Wyman Ltd.
Production - Oval Projects Ltd.

The Bluffer's Guides are based on
an original idea by Peter Wolfe.

INTRODUCTION

Jazz is a good subject for bluffing in because whoever happens to contradict you is almost certainly bluffing as well. This is because nobody seems to know the basic answers as to how, where or why it all began. So your theories are as good as anyone else's.

You may also hold the most outrageous critical opinions (e.g. that Bunk Johnson was a skilled trumpet player or that Jelly Roll Morton was a modest man) and the jazz world, far from regarding you as a loon, will respect your viewpoint and earnestly discuss the basis of your contentions.

However, there are three notes of caution. The earnest jazz enthusiast is as earnest as anyone you will ever have met, so:

1. Never make jokes about jazz; or, at least, make them with a straight face.

2. Whatever line you take, stick to it – no matter where it may lead you.

3. Don't agree with anyone completely. Concur occasionally in moderate mutual admiration of the art of Dink Johnson (or whoever crops up) but make sure that it is for different reasons. Total agreement will only lead to a reputation for indifference.

The advantage of jazz over other kinds of music is that you don't have to listen to it if you don't want to. If that sounds unduly cynical let us assure you that plenty of people who do listen to it don't actually *listen* to it either. While the music is being played, live or on record, they are arguing, very loudly, about how – or even if – the contents of rare and crackling old 78s should be transferred to cassette or compact disc. They are questioning whether Russell Davies/ Richard Cook/Leonard Feather/Brian Rust, or any other jazz presenter/editor/columnist/authority knows what he is talking about.

They are pontificating on exactly when Louis Armstrong stopped being great, why Miles Davis was the way he was, what Anthony Braxton's geometric titles really mean; and why it isn't jazz if there is no banjo. They are asking whoever is sitting next to them which two *Blue Note* sleeves were designed by Andy Warhol.

This chatter ceases only during a bass solo when it is suddenly apparent that everything has gone comparatively quiet; or during a drum solo when it is generally too noisy even to hear yourself bicker. We are sure that you'd like to join in all this innocent fun and there is no reason why not.

Never mind that you've always assumed a middle eight to be a boat race crew or that you believe Ruby Braff to be a female wrestler and Randy Brecker a kind of muesli. Ignorance has never deterred others for a second and in this kind of verbal warfare he who hesitates is bossed. So, with this little book, get in there and start pontificating too.

PURE JAZZ

The glorious thing about jazz is that there is neither a universally accepted definition of the word nor a factually provable account of the music's origins. Thus on these two points at least you say whatever comes into your head and, jazz talk being what it is, the crankier the better.

If you want to maintain, for instance, that the word 'jazz' is simply a corruption of 'jars' – this based on the fact that an improvised, percussive sort of music was first played by the people of what became The Gambia striking (with dried vulture bones – always be specific on points like this as it adds conviction) glass jars washed ashore after a consignment of Cooper's Oxford Marmalade went down off West Africa in 1756 – well, go ahead. Few will dare argue against such detailed knowledge.

Or if you feel like suggesting that the word 'jazz' is derived from the black American word 'jizz' meaning horizontal exercise, then there's nothing to stop you. Unless you happen to be talking to someone like Paul Oliver or Tony Russell or Samuel B. Charters, who will have embarked on some even more abstruse theory before you can get a word in.

Then there is the music itself. You will possibly have wondered about those bass and drum solos – especially if you come from other musical areas where those who play such instruments know their place. In jazz, alas, bass-players and drummers have long established the right to indulge in solo displays, generally of unforgivable length and tediousness.

There were several reasons for this, but the main and most practical reason is that of all members of a jazz group the bass player and the drummer, simply on account of the bulky nature of the tools of their trade, were the most likely to possess their own transport. So the other members of the band were beholden to these two when it came to getting a lift home after the gig. Fear of being stranded outweighed artistic sensibility and forced them to condone an inordinate amount of plucking and bashing – even at the cost of their own rightful solo time.

Such matters may seem to be of an unduly prosaic nature, but the jazz life tended and still tends to be one of down-to-earth practicalities. It is best to be warned here and now not to try any jazz bluffing on genuine jazz musicians. None of them are the least bothered with the Gambian theory of the origins of jazz. All that concerns them is the chord sequence and the Musicians Union rates for the job.

Kinds of Jazz

There are two kinds of Jazz:

Traditional – Jazz played in the old three-up three-down style, mostly a collective improvisation on *When the Saints go marching in*.

Modern – Jazz conceived and recorded since 1940.

It is not actually possible, though many critics try to do it, to like or support both Trad and Mod. It is like saying that you support both the Conservative and Labour parties at the same time. So decide which you uphold and decry the other on every occasion; or, if you can't make up your mind what you like, say you prefer:

Mainstream – The term invented to cover middle-of-the-road Liberal sort of jazz.

This was thought up one restless night by the eminent critic Stanley Fosdick Dance after he had spent an evening at a jam session featuring **Duke Ellington** with members of his band, **Brad Gowans**, **Horsecollar Draper** and **Eddie Condon**. At a loss for words to describe what he had heard he tried to dignify the proceedings by calling it 'mainstream'.

Jazz History

Jazz is too young (compared with institutions such as pawnbroking and opera) to have much history; but it has nonetheless acquired a quite disproportionate body of myth, fable and legend. If it were not for a few solid and unassailable facts like **Fats Waller**, **Pinetop Smith**'s death certificate, **Ronnie Scott**'s Club, and **Thelonious Monk**'s version of *Nice work if you can get it*, one might suspect that the jazz press had made the whole thing up.

In reality, only 75 per cent of it was made up, chiefly by **Jelly Roll Morton** with a few inept contributions from **Bunk Johnson** and *Jazzmen*.

One of Morton's most helpful myths was that he personally invented jazz on March 2nd, 1902. If we'd had the sense to go along with his claim, jazz would now have a concise, tidy history, leaving us free to listen to the music. Jazz history books would have been able to divide events neatly into AM and PM – after Morton and pre-Morton. There would be fewer post-Mortons on jazz than there have been.

Above all, the history of jazz is names – not so much a narrative as a roll-call from **Irving Aaronson** to **Mike Zwerin**. In between, just to keep it interesting and to make it harder for newcomers to crack the code, are numerous characters, many of whom probably didn't exist at all.

You might like to keep in conversational reserve someone like **Stavin Chain**, a figure so marginal as to be practically off the page. Elsewhere we offer a fine bargain selection of names such as **Nesuhi Ertegun**, **Eustern Woodfork**, **Hociel T. Tebo**, **John Fallstich**, **Wim Poppink** and **Cornelius Plumb**. You may logically choose to disbelieve all of these. So do we, but they have all been seen on the backs of quite respectable record sleeves.

The name that is totally unavoidable in jazz history is **Jelly Roll Morton** about whom it is imperative to know several basic things – such as that he was a pimp, a gambler, a pool shark, and a small-time hustler involved in a lot of dubious enterprises; and that he had a diamond set into one of his front teeth.

His given first name was Ferdinand (and his original surname was Lamothe or Le Menthe, which he changed to Morton because he didn't like being called 'Frenchy') but he acquired the nickname of 'Jelly Roll' which like 90 per cent of all names and words used in jazz has connections with sexual rather than musical prowess*. The common supposition is that Morton was rather good at it. But his widow recalled, somewhere or other, that he was not particularly outstanding in this department.

---

* In the 30s, pained to learn of the sexual connotations of Morton's name the BBC suggested that, if his records had to be played at all, then he should be referred to as J.R. Morton.

Only after you've absorbed all this vital information need you consider certain irrelevancies – e.g. that he was one of the first musicians to compose pieces specifically for jazz performance; that he was a superb, if somewhat prissy piano player and a very skilled bandleader; and that while he irritated people with his boasting, he irritated them even more by proving that much of what he bragged about was true.

Moreover he did it all (hear him on those famous interviews with Alan Lomax) with the charm of a real old Southern gentleman, right out of some TV soap opera, that much belied his nickname.

He was born in New Orleans and suffered all his life from a rare disease known as Spanish tinge. He lied about his age, but the wrong way to the conventional one. It seems to have been a common trait in old jazz musicians. He let people assume he'd been born in 1885 which got him among Ragtime goings-on. It wasn't until the 100th anniversary celebrations were in full swing in 1985 that fresh research suggested that his true birth-date was 1890. This meant that Jelly (use the familiar form whenever you can) could be the subject of two centenary celebrations only five years apart. Another to add to his list of unique achievements.

Others, like **Bunk Johnson** (*q.v.*), got everyone so effectively confused by phoney birth-dates that he threw the whole of jazz history out of order by getting a few eager pioneer historians to believe him. The mess is only just being sorted out by learned gentlemen in various American universities.

You see now why it doesn't matter all that much if you throw in a few dubious facts now and then. Jazz history is insecurely based on the art of misinformation.

11

Up the River and All That Jazz

Nevertheless, it is always a good thing to have a few firm facts on hand, so here goes:

Jazz was invented in New Orleans c.17th November 1887. It was created by a creole barber's assistant called **Thermidus Brown**, known to his acquaintances and his admirers as 'Jazz-bo' on account of his snappy dressing. It just happened one night c.1 a.m., when Thermidus was tootling around with a theme on a battered cornet that he had bought in 1867 from an ex-Civil war bandsman called Ephraim Draper. Being, as he always was by 1 a.m., totally under the influence of home-brewed rye whisky, Thermidus began to mistime his phrases in a way that gave the tune a strangely propulsive sort of quality. This greatly excited the customers in 'Loopy' Dumaine's lakeside crawfish restaurant (popularly known as 'Loopy's Place') where he was playing at the time. Later, the professors were to define what he was doing as syncopation. To Thermidus it was simply an inner memory of the banjo rhythms from the old plantation where he served his time as a slave in his younger days.

We know little of Thermidus. Almost everything that is known about him is the fact that his father was a black mule-breaker called Brown, that he was born in New Orleans c.1847, and that on 5 July 1894 in an intoxicated state (soon after 2 a.m.) he was drowned when he fell off a riverboat on his way up river to St. Louis, where he was going to invent Ragtime.*

* Most of these facts were revealed by pianist 'Precious' Clarence Turner in an interview he gave before he died in 1967, soon after recording his only LP 'Boogie-Woogie Explosions' (Saga SOC1041).

The exciting new sounds that Thermidus created that evening soon spread among the local dance band musicians and by 1897 or so were to be heard everywhere in New Orleans, notably being played by the ex-editor of a scandal-sheet known as *The Cricket* (rare copies of which now fetch as much as $5,000), one **Charles 'Buddy' Bolden**, often credited on radio quizzes as the originator of jazz.

Bolden's main claim to fame was the loudness of his playing; it being said, with the straightest of faces, that he could be heard 'fourteen miles away on a clear night'. As nobody who was fourteen miles away at the time has ever come forward to verify this, it is yet another jazz legend that has to be treated with a modicum of suspicion.

The would-be jazz bluffer may already sense the deep under-currents of blarney that lie beneath the surface of jazz history. The options are to express an unshakeable belief in these legends (a standpoint taken by many writers of jazz books); or to condemn them as being obviously ridiculous (as difficult an argument to uphold as trying to maintain that Noah never built an ark).

The next thing that happened to jazz, was that it went up the river. Again only the faintest vestiges of the truth have been hinted at here. The fact is that an unscrupulous individual with the doom-laden name of **Fate Marable** who had come from Paducah and was a third-rate exponent of the steam calliope (an inefficient instrument which suffered – as you can see in old silent films – from leaky valves), began to feel that New Orleans was getting over-crowded with jazz musicians. Especially the good ones like Louis Armstrong.

So, for a modest sum, he bought himself the right to

act as a sort of employment agent for hiring jazz musicians to play riverboats that plied up and down the Mississippi.

He paid them enough to tempt them to make the journey up to far-flung places like St. Louis knowing that they would never be able to afford to get back. Which left things much better for him in New Orleans. He would lure them with posters that made Chicago look like a bracing seaside town and off they would go hoping to find fame and fortune with a one-way ticket in one hand and an instrument case in the other. None of them knew that, back home in Paducah, he had once run a travel agency.

Ragtime

The theory, first propounded by Theolosiphus J. Elfleikmann Jr. II in 'Ragtime Re-Defined: a Collection of Papers Read at the University of Milneburg, July 7-15, 1943' that Ragtime was first invented in Fred's Eating House on West 37th Street, St. Louis, because the pianist had hiccups, is now considered untenable. Nor does the assumption that it happened in a shoot-out in the office of a publisher of player-piano rolls (see *Fourteen Miles on a Clear Night*) now seem anything but far-fetched. In fact, it seemed far-fetched even then and several critics did not hesitate to say so.

On the other hand the story put forward by a well-known anonymous writer in the *Saint Louis Post-Dispatch* that it was invented by a black woman called Mrs. Danbury in 1888 has to be taken with a pinch of salt. The truth probably lies somewhere in the midst of all this. Most likely it was the result of using a piano which had several keys that didn't play. There were a lot of them around at the time, second-hand ex-gold rush stock, many of them badly shot up.

It is possible and advisable to adopt a particularly purist attitude toward ragtime. It is the one jazz-oriented subject that the general musical conversationalist is likely to veer toward on the strength of having seen a film called *The Sting*. Unlike most jazz, ragtime actually exists in printed scores, and, for some, these have become the Gospel according to St. Joshua.

What you must do is put an end to people thinking that because they own a **Joshua Rifkin** record they know all about it. Rifkin, as most will know, was an American musicologist, a specialist in medieval music and sometime jug-blower, who had the bright idea of playing and recording Joplin straight.

Unfortunately this made ragtime accessible to anybody. The ragtime specialist will therefore find it politic to cast aspersions on Rifkin's so-called purity. You will suspect that genuine ragtime purveyors would not have sounded (or even looked) like that at all. Apart from the fact that they would have been playing a shot-up ex-gold-rush model rather than a Steinway; would not have been wearing tails; might even have smiled; and would probably have been well tanked-up with whatever was going free in the alcohol line, they would, you should say, have played in a much freer style.

Max Morath (who generally wears a bowler-hat – often a sign of authenticity*), a good name to use, is

---

* Many early musicians of impeachable obscurity wore bowlers or derbies. The custom was mainly established, however, by Willie 'The Lion' Smith, a player noted for his bravery. Like all the rules it has its exceptions, e.g. Acker Bilk.

probably nearer to the 'jig' style of **Tom Turpin**. A handful of such names can easily be culled from books like *Ragtime Rarities* edited by Trebor Jay Tichenor (which is a genuine name in daily use in America).

You might make a start with **Harvey M. Babcock**, **Mattie Harl Burgess**, **E. Warren Furry**, **J. Bodewalt Lampe**, **Julia Lee Niebergall** or **Frank X. McFadden**. Jot them down somewhere. Most of these, casually trotted out, could easily take the wind out of the sails of even an established ragtime know-all.

The name of **Scott Joplin** (1868-1917) has become almost contemptibly familiar. Any attempts to bandy his name about as the only one that really matters in ragtime should immediately be rebuffed by dark suggestions that **James Scott**, **Arthur Marshall**, **Joe Jordan** and so on, were actually superior. Untrue but tenable, and few will have done the necessary groundwork to be able to argue.

Joplin established a few of the unshakable tenets of ragtime like *'Notice! Don't play this piece fast. It is never right to play 'Ragtime' fast. Author'* – a sort of government health warning he had printed on many of his pieces. In spite of this he made his name with a work called *Maple Leaf rag* which he (amongst many) always played at a high rate of knots.

Joplin was very ambitious and got fixed on the idea of writing a ragtime opera which he called *Treemonisha*. He spent all his well-earned royalties on it and his failure to get it produced finally drove him insane. Had he lived as long as **Eubie Blake***, he would almost have seen the days when *Treemonisha* was put on in a

---

* Eubie Blake, when interviewed at the age of 100 not long before he died, said: 'If I'd known I was going to live so long I'd have taken better care of myself' (he was a regular smoker and drinker).

respectable opera house and recorded by a German recording company; and the rest of his music freely making money in the shape of film-scores, ballets and commercial jingles.

You will have to gauge very carefully the strength of the conversational competition but, if you think you can do it without getting caught, by all means hint that you know quite a bit about **Louis Moreau Gottschalk** (1829-69). Born in New Orleans he became a virtuoso pianist – people compared him with Liszt – and a prolific composer, some of whose works, based on Louisiana folk dances, do have an extraordinary ragtime-like flavour. If you feel like being really contentious you might try arguing that he was the true begetter of ragtime.

The Blues

The blues are so intrinsic to jazz that you really don't have to say much about them. In any case, musicologically speaking, there is not really all that much to say. They all have the same tune and the same chord sequence and are all played at the same speed. The words, when sung, are more or less the same – on the lines of:

'Woke up dis mornin' with an awful aching head
Woke up dis mornin' with an awful aching head
My man (or woman) done gone left me
And I wish that I was dead.'

The words are freely shouted or incanted in a rough sort of voice and the very best blues singers become less and less decipherable as the verses proceed. This helps to create work for scholarly commentators.

To be considered an authority on the blues you should at least have spoken (even if it was only to say 'hello') to Paul Oliver. He is the author of most of the books that have been written on the blues and has been to Africa as well as the Deep South of America.

If you are setting yourself up as a real blues expert you should not be discussing anybody who was actually commercially successful in this field (e.g. **Bessie Smith,** so-called Empress of the Blues, or even **Ma Rainey**) or recorded with jazz musicians. If you once had a liking for **Josh White**, just don't mention it. No – real blues singers, the deeply incomprehensible, all have names like Blind Willie, Deaf Tom, One-Armed Alex or Luther Rainshine. A few of the better-known ones who sang in an authentically incomprehensible way like **Blind Lemon Jefferson** or **Leadbelly**, are also perfectly acceptable.

The ideal blues singer* is physically and vocally handicapped and will, at most, have recorded one item called *Black-hearted blues No. 5* which was on the obscure and unobtainable Krapp label; the only copy of which has see-through grooves and is owned by a reclusive collector in Bournemouth.

Credit for inventing the blues was claimed by a black Memphis bandmaster called **W. C. Handy**; but this has long been disregarded. At most he gets credit for the neat idea of always having tunes that are 12-bars long, so that anyone can tell they are blues, and

---

* His tombstone, should he have one, would be inscribed with the words 'Didn't wake up this morning'. Or, perhaps:

> 'This is the grave of Two-Note Jake
> Who, this morning, failed to wake.'

for the 'Woke up this mornin' with an awful aching head' (repeated twice) syndrome.

Anyone looking for a clear definition of the blues, even in the most scholarly books, will be told that blues are fundamentally a state of mind. The spirit of the blues inhabits all true jazz. It's what makes it 'funky'.

Boogie-Woogie

The blues translated to piano goes under various descriptions – barrelhouse, honky-tonk, etc., all titles descriptive of low-class origins and environment. It is somewhat embarrassing to the scholarly interpreter of jazz meaning, who is himself generally a blameless soul addicted to nothing more sinister than a glass of shandy and sandals, to find that nearly all the basic jazz jargon derives from sexual activities.

'Boogie', as decent souls will know, is a Southern name for a prostitute; and 'boogie-woogie' was the secondary stage of syphilis. Hence much of the boogie-woogie that became fashionable in the 1930s had perverted sexual titles like *Beat me, daddy, eight to the bar* or *Honky-tonk train blues*.

Boogie-woogie, basically twelve-bar variations over a regular figured bass, ranges from the sparse tinkerings of bluesey **Jimmy Yancey** to the pounding ebullience of **Pete Johnson** & **Albert Ammons** who must have got through two pianos a week. It inspired similar thunderous swing band versions (that got through two loud-speakers a week) and became a basic ingredient of that early manifestation of pop known as 'rock 'n' roll'.

Swing

It is generally accepted now that the word swing came into jazz from the world of sex, drugs and hamburgers. The lady, one **Delia 'Sugar' Brown**, who first cried out 'Oh, swing it' to her man was not actually referring to the music, though the fact that he was dancing with nothing on at the time may have helped the connection. In South-West Alabama, those who could 'swing it' were generally considered to be physically well-endowed in one way or another. The term gradually came to be applied to the kind of music that was inclined to set things in motion. Eventually to a kind of big-band jazz that laid particular emphasis on a propulsive beat.

It is generally considered that **Duke Ellington** put swing on the map when he wrote a controversial little number called *It don't mean a thing if it ain't got that swing* in 1931. This, of course, greatly upset those who had got along without it very well for several decades, and many thought that the coming of swing was the end of genuine jazz.

The name was subsequently and thereafter taken up by the biggish bands who wanted some word to describe what they were doing apart from providing the background for dancing and making money. Swing bands were much looked down upon by early jazz enthusiasts but age has now made them acceptable. **Benny Goodman** was crowned the 'King of Swing' by his agent (who was on 25 per cent) and was the first jazzman to attract huge adolescent crowds, later referred to as 'bobby-soxers'.

Swing itself, having been buried c.1946, became respectable and collectable and much sold in pirated recordings taken from the radio.

New Orleans Jazz

A taste for New Orleans jazz is the equivalent of liking (in the classical field) the sound of crumhorns, rebecs and lutes or (in literature) of enjoying Beowulf. It is always a good thing in any contentious area of discussions like jazz to be an avowed purist. The purest of all purists in the jazz field is the staunch supporter of New Orleans jazz, he who maintains that New Orleans jazz is the only righteous stuff.

In view of the obvious improvements in techniques that have happened since, it is not an easy position to hold. But, basically, the tenets are that:

1. Everything should be played in B flat (a possible diversion now and then into F or E flat but not to be overdone);

2. Everything should be played in an undeviating 2/4;

3. There should only be one of each instrument, these being the cornet, the clarinet and the trombone (designated the front-line); the banjo, tuba and drums (being the rhythm-section); and a piano (providing it is hard of tone and slightly out of tune).

NB: it must be cornet (a battered one to boot) and never a trumpet. That is the first unbreakable law, the second and third being that it must be a banjo and not a guitar, a tuba and not a string-bass.

New Orleans bands spent half their time performing in low dives where the pianos matured nicely on a diet of spilled alcohol; the other half marching down the streets of New Orleans as background music to funerals. On the way to the graveyard they played, as was only right, slowly and mournfully. On the way back they played fast so as not to waste any time in getting to the hostelry.

The decrepit state of their instruments and the decrepit state of the players who all drank heavily or smoked marijuana, tended to give genuine New Orleans jazz the flavour of fried boots. Its general decrepitude was perhaps exaggerated in the 1940s when there was a revival of interest in the real thing and now ancient musicians, minus such useful assets as teeth and memories, were provided with suitably battered instruments and sparked off a fanatical interest in the trad sound.

Anyone not knowing the above requirements of New Orleans jazz might well have taken the records they bought of such revival bands back to the shop thinking there was something technically wrong with them. The connoisseur would, on the other hand, have revelled in the cracked notes, savoured the rare ability to play just off-key (difficult to do deliberately), and admired the elephantine rhythm with the unique flavour that comes from the intermingling of plinked banjo and plonked bass.

Once the original New Orleans jazz musicians had blown themselves out and eventually expired, there was nothing else to be done except produce faithful imitations. This was rarely attempted by young black musicians who had turned to much more cerebral things (see Minton's), but generally by a breed of bibulous white musicians whose main affinity with the originals was that they could knock back a pint or two.

The American ones had fine names like the **Yerba Buena Jazz Band** and the **State Street Stompers** while the British ones, lacking these affiliations but sensing that rivers were essential to jazz concocted names like the **Crane River Jazz Band** and the **Kennett and Avon Canal Footwarmers**.

Chicago Jazz

Once Fate Marable had fleeced them of their fares up river, most jazzmen got off the boat somewhere around St. Louis, bought a hamburger with what they had left, then hitched a lift to Chicago. So many jazz musicians were blowing themselves silly in Chicago in the 1920s it became known as the Windy City.

The black musicians were mainly employed by one **Joe Oliver**, known as 'King' Oliver because he had got there first. Oliver formed a group which he called his **Creole Jazz Band** (although it didn't seem to have any creoles in it) and sent for an up-and-coming young cornettist called **Louis Armstrong** to join him.

The first great jazz innovation was seen when the band, playing New Orleans sort of stuff, appeared with two cornets. The purists see this as the first step in the decline of jazz and toward the unfortunate excesses of the Swing Era. But the far-seeing bluffer, should latch on to this and possibly start an argument about which bits Armstrong played and which bits Oliver took. The pre-electric quality of the recording makes it hard to tell, so it is a good area in which to turn hypothesis into bold assertion, in true bluffing tradition.

The other brand of Chicago jazz was that which was purveyed by white musicians either by:

a) some professionals who modelled themselves on Oliver and called themselves the **New Orleans Rhythm Kings**, or

b) some young lads just out of short trousers who modelled themselves on the New Orleans Rhythm Kings and called themselves the **Chicagoans**.

Not having the physical capacity of the regulars they found the New Orleans style of playing, where everybody kept going all the time, a little taxing. So they invented a new Chicago style where they each took turns to play solos while the others had a drink or a drag, only combining briefly at the beginning and the end of a number.

Some of them, like **Pee Wee Russell**, evolved very economical styles with a minimum of notes. As most of the jazz haunts were boozing spots run by such pushing businessmen as Al Capone and his henchmen, the jazz musicians did all right if they just kept playing and ignored the shooting.

New York Jazz

For various reasons, such as having a difference of opinion with Al Capone, jazz musicians gradually drifted towards the city known as the Big Apple (because everyone wanted to have a bite out of it) – New York. So many black folk arrived that they took over most of the Northern bit of Manhattan called Harlem – and that's where jazz started (according to the stance that you adopt) either to decline or mature. Not only did they have two cornets but they now played trumpets, sometimes three or four of them; and (whisper it not in Purity Street) *saxophones*, hundreds of them. The saxophone gradually came to epitomise jazz and got it a bad name in conservative circles. Saxophones did not just blow or get blown, they honked and wailed and slapped and upset all right-thinking folk.

The dustcart ensembles of New Orleans and the

neurotic amateurism of the Chicagoans were ironed out in New York. The black musicians played a sort of 'mainstream' jazz long before the word was invented. It was a more professional kind of music in which all the musicians played cleverly (i.e. wandered beyond the three basic chords) and quite fast. Someone from Kansas City (*q.v.*) dropped in and showed them what a riff was so they were all very happy. **Coleman Hawkins**, the famous tenor-saxophonist, later said that he didn't think there was any distinctive New York style and, so far as what was played in Harlem was concerned, he was right.

But there was another sort of New York jazz that was played by the young white musicians who had come up in **Frankie Trumbauer**'s car from Chicago. This was a stultified form of Chicago jazz played in a jerky sort of way that was much copied by British dance bands. The New York bands had names like **Miff Mole and his Little Molers**, **Red Nichols and his Five Pennies** and, just to confuse the editors of *Jazzmen* even more, the **Original Memphis Five**, the **Charleston Chasers**, the **Louisiana Rhythm Kings**, the **Tennessee Tooters**, the **Savannah Six**, and the **Cotton Pickers**. Not to mention **Gene Fosdick's Hoosiers** – as most jazz histories have not done before us.

Kansas City Jazz

This was rather like black New York jazz except that they were hooked on riffs. A riff is when you find a phrase you like, usually played by a whole section or the entire band, so you keep on playing it in a compulsively propulsive sort of way throughout the piece. The idea came one day when the needle got stuck in a groove and they all thought it was quite a novel effect.

Kansas City jazz was mainly run by a chap called **Bennie Moten**, later succeeded by **Count Basie** who kept the riff tradition going strong for many lucrative years. A later band was run by **Jay McShann**, remembered in jazz history because **Charlie Parker** had his first reed trouble within its ranks.

Minton's

Minton's Playhouse – which you will always succinctly refer to as Minton's – was in a disused china warehouse on West 118th Street in Harlem. A Christian sect (believers in **Charlie Christian** the guitarist, that is) began to hold meetings there about 1940, after they had reached the conviction that the sort of jazz people could understand easily and could dance to and enjoy had been going on long enough; and it was time something was done about it.

To be fair that wasn't actually Charlie Christian's own philosophy; he was quite content simply to be the best jazz guitarist ever and to play for his own pleasure at every opportunity, even if it was with a big commercial band. To that end he dispensed with all inessentials, including sleep, and was dead by 1942, thus providing another of the great dividing lines in jazz history – B.C: Before Christian.

Everything later than that is, of course, A.D, standing for After Dizzy, **Dizzy Gillespie** being perhaps the most important of all the Minton's habitués.

26

Another was **Kenny Clarke** who had a way of whacking the bass drum at moments in the music when people were least expecting it. This made him very famous and, since war was just becoming fashionable again, the practice was known as dropping bombs.

Besides creating a boom (in the other sense) in the sale and repair of bass drum pedals, it put older musicians off their stroke (or beat), which was what some historians claim was the whole object of those sessions at Minton's. Kenny Clarke's bomb-dropping and the very complex harmonics and chords that Dizzy Gillespie and Thelonious Monk worked out, together with the frantic tempos all the young musicians would indulge in, were believed to be part of a deliberate plan to drive non-progressive musicians (like Louis Armstrong and all those white players like Goodman who were making a lot of money out of jazz) off the stand. The fact that this has often been denied by those involved, lends great weight and authority to the theory.

Thelonious Monk was such a weird cat that even other weird cats noticed it. His name, to start with, seems to have been partially created by himself, for there is evidence to suggest that his given first name was Thelius (which would have been odd enough for some people) and that his middle name, Sphere, was entirely of his own manufacture. He had a very accessible, completely beguiling and rather humorous style of playing which would occasionally take on the characteristics of ye olde stride piano with a sort of limp.

Many of the more academically correct pianists in jazz used to say that Monk couldn't play; so you can tell from that how extremely good and important he really was. He wore strange hats, had a wife named

Nellie who cut his fingernails, and used words like 'crepuscule'.

Charlie Parker was a frequent sitter-in at Minton's but he wasn't strictly a Mintonian since his style had developed quite independently, largely in people's woodsheds and from listening to slowed-down Lester Young records. Nevertheless Parker's presence on the scene was a great advantage because it has since given every musician who was around at that time the chance to claim that Charlie Parker once shared a room with him.

In fact, it's a pretty safe bet, if an unfamiliar 1940s/50s name crops up in conversation, that you can easily get away with saying: "Oh, yes. Parker roomed with him for a time." Even if he didn't, nobody is going to be sure enough to say so. And it somehow makes the unknown musician seem a better player.

To sum up: Minton's was the place where modern jazz was invented. The fact that nearly 50 years have gone by since it happened means that it isn't strictly modern at all. But, just as in history the Middle Ages aren't anywhere near the middle, so in jazz the nomenclatures tend to slip a bit. This is to everyone's advantage, since it offers limitless opportunities to argue over what to call everything that has happened ever since.

Into The Cool

What Cole Porter said about a crêpe suzette, holds good for jazz as well: it was too hot not to cool down. The wonder is, in fact, that jazz managed to stay hot for as long as it did. In New Orleans it was kept at a steady 86°F (34° Boyd Sentergrade) – not difficult down there since the state of Louisiana was part of Dixie where, if it's true what they say, the sun really shines all the time.

Nor was it any problem making sure it stayed piping hot on the long trip up the river. Jazz was stowed next to the boiler-room and, in any case, the Streckfus Brothers and Fate Marable between them crammed so many passengers, dancers, gamblers and other revellers aboard the riverboats that these fantastic vessels (to quote the Mississippi historian Marshall Stearnwheel) 'were not so much pleasure steamers as floating armpits'.

Even when it got to the windy city of Chicago, jazz remained a hot property in every sense. Another reason why Chicago was called the Windy City was that most of the inhabitants were terrified of the gangsters, particularly Al (short for Alcohol) Capone. The rival gangs, having installed hot and cold running meths in every room, would make gin in their bath-tubs, beer in the garage, and an Italian house wine, called Maffietto, in army surplus wellingtons (hence the name 'bootleg').

It was the aim of each gang to hold a monopoly on the supply of these illegal but nutritious beverages. To that end they shot each other and anybody else who looked as if they might know the secret of fermentation – on sight. Jazz musicians are born knowing the secret of fermentation, so, in order to keep alive, they had to present a constantly moving target. Neither they nor the music, therefore, had a chance to settle for a minute. This kept Chicago jazz hot and gave it its agitated character.

Its temperature couldn't be brought down straight away even when it had got to north-easterly New York.

Anyone who has ever seen a film shot in New York knows that even the tiniest crack in the New York City sidewalk has steam coming out of it. The basements in which jazz flourished in the 30s and 40s (**The Three Juices**, **The Sardonyx**, **The Chicory House** to name hardly any) were thus stifling and jazz, once again, had little chance to get cooled to the point where it was fit for the table.

In 1949 it was decided that if jazz (which had been called 'hot' music since even before Jelly Roll Morton dreamed that he had invented it in 1902) was not disposed to obey the law of thermodynamics* of its own accord, then it must be made to do so.

The result was one of the two things in the history of the world ever to be successfully brought about by a committee. The first was the King James Bible, the second was the convincing of the general public that jazz, like dry sherry, ought to be served chilled.

The following are names that you must toss into any discussion of this aspect of jazz: **Gil Evans** (born in Canada – another useful card to have up your sleeve); **John Lewis** (who would later invent the **Modern Jazz Quartet** and who dressed in a manner that would have been approved of by Lord Reith); **Gerry Mulligan** (who invented the Gerry Mulligan Quartet and has a tendency to dress like Hamlet) and **Johnny Carisi** (a trumpet player who had never been heard of before and has never been seen since). They were the Cooling Committee. To it they co-opted **Miles Davis** who immediately took over and became the dominant element in the 9-piece band specially assembled for Operation Frigidaire.

* The heat of the music is in inverse proportion to the detachment of the player.

The band was booked for two weeks into a place called the Royal Roast. In view of its declared aims this name was felt to be something of an ill omen, and the management was persuaded to change it to the Royal Roost, which explains how this otherwise inexplicable name came into the history books. Casually referred to as the **Royal Roost** band (use the name at every opportunity) it did a couple of recording sessions, and when the results were put together, the album was called *Into the Cool* so that there should be absolutely no mistake about what they were trying to do.

Thus was founded the cool school and pupils hurried to enrol. One of its housemasters was blind pianist **Lennie Tristano** who taught the joint head prefects of the school, the alto-saxophonist **Lee Konitz** and the tenor-saxophonist **Warne Marsh** whose first name was a clever amalgamation of 'wan' and 'worn', both of which he sounded.

Soon after, this cool school opened up a branch in California, paradoxically because the weather was warmer there. That got it called West Coast jazz and it gave jazz people an interesting topic, discussing whether West Coast jazz was cooler and more intellectual than the East Coast variety.

Meanwhile, inevitably, a reaction had set in, and a much hotter form of cool jazz was started up called hard bop, because it was hard to play and, for some people, even harder to listen to. Hard bop musicians included the drummer **Art Blakey** who had metal studs, which were named after him, nailed to the bottom of his boots. This was the beginning of sole music.

As time has gone by, so it has become more apparent that many of the cool players were in reality pretty hot while several of the hard boppers were real cool and cognizant – a pretty cerebral lot. In fact, the further you get away from the 50s and 60s the harder it becomes to see what all the fuss was about; leaving you to wonder, once again, if it was the writers who started a lot of jazz history as a precaution against redundancy.

Furthermore, if there's ever a lull in the conversation you can always get it going again by pointing out that the first cool jazz musician was actually **Bix Beiderbecke**, in the late 20s, but everybody was too busy enjoying the music and dodging Al Capone to notice it at the time.

Le Jazz Hot

Une chose très comique regardent les French est qu'ils avaient beaucoup de difficulté in trouving les mots propre of their own pour les choses comme hot jazz qui sounds stupide si vous l'appellez le jazz chaude.

A une fois ils appelerent ragtime 'le temps du chiffon' qui est pourquoi il ne catch on pas pour une longtemps. Comme en Angleterre le majorité de jazz est joué en Londres, en France le majorité de jazz est joué à Paris. Oo la la.

Pour une longtemps il était mostly **Django Reinhardt**, un guitarist romanesque avec des doigts missing, et un fiddler nomme de **Stephane Grappelly** qui jouaient avec un combination qui s'appelle **Le Quintette du Hot Club de France**.

Le Président du Hot Club de France était **Hugues Panassié** qui dit que tout le jazz après 1940 n'était pas le jazz véritable avec l'exception de les sessions qu'il organisé soi-même. Quelques-uns dites 'bon vieux Hugues', mais les autres dites 'testicles'.

A Paris, en les clubs très expensive, une organisé par une femme célèbre nomme de **Bricktop**, vous could trouvez après le Guerre Deuxième du Mond les musiciens comme **Mezz Mezzrow**, **Sidney Bechet**, **Bill Coleman**, **Kenny Clarke** et des modernes prolifiques.

Tout le Jazz traditionel français sounded comme Sidney Bechet. Tout le Jazz modern français sounded comme rien sur le mond. Qui est pourquoi les musiciens americains étaient si populair à Paris. Oo la la.

British Jazz

Jazz – as you might well expect – took quite a while to catch on in the British Isles. In fact, there are still areas in the extreme Celtic fringes where it has not really got a foothold nor ousted the native music. It was not simply because it was black: the Victorians had always had a high regard for the minstrel shows and had welcomed to their shores the followers of the great Christy. In the first place, it had to overcome so many rooted ideas and tribal customs. Things like Promenade Concerts, the Bath Pumproom and the Palm Courts, the Band of the Grenadier Guards and all those brass bands blasting away in the North, the Music Hall, Gilbert & Sullivan and Hymns Ancient and Modern.

In the second place jazz turned out to be a bit low-class. The American practitioners who crossed the Atlantic proved to be a rough lot and drank heavily. Early British jazz was played by working-class Jewish lads from Whitechapel and beyond, who drank even more. Its prominent figures included a trumpeter called **Nat Gonella** who couldn't even sound his r's.

There were those who tried to instil a bit of polish like **Henry Hall** who dressed and spoke immaculately; and there was a chap called **Featherstonaugh**, but, in spite of their best endeavours, British polite society, particularly vicars and councillors, were horrified at the sounds which jazz made. They were particularly upset by the saxophone. Mr Clutsam, who was an authority on the strength of having written *Lilac Time*, cheered everybody up by predicting it would never last; while Mr George Robey (who had been up-staged by the **Original Dixieland Jazz Band**) said that it was ruining family life.

Around the late forties jazz slowly began to catch on, although it had a brief setback when one leading revivalist called **George Webb** was seen to play the piano with his braces showing. It was at this point, however, that the press discovered that one of its leading trumpeters, **Humphrey Lyttelton**, had not only been a Guards officer but had been to Eton. It became the thing for the bowler-hatted brigade to swear allegiance to jazz on the strength of their identical qualifications. From now on jazz was eminently respectable and one of the arts; a multitude of books were written about it. There were setbacks from time to time like the Beaulieu riots and **George Melly** but, on the whole, British jazz was decent and hard-working and quite like the real thing.

Modern jazz came to Britain in the most romantic way. In the late 40s, a few Charlie Parker records arrived as ballast aboard a tramp steamer. Secretly meeting in cellars and West End flats where the curtains were permanently drawn, young London-based musicians like **John Dankworth** (never call him 'Johnny'), **Ronnie Scott** (always call him 'Ronnie') and **Tony Crombie** listened to these records and underwent immediate religious conversion. Their shrine was 52nd Street, New York, and in order to make the pilgrimage they signed on as unable seamen in Geraldo's Navy, **Geraldo** being the Fate Marable of the transatlantic liners. They brought back Bop, as music and also as a way of life, on their return trips. So jazz, which had run out of rivers to go up, now put to sea; still travelling steerage, of course.

On June 2, 1974 the phrase 'do your own thing' was coined by an uncredited writer and a new generation of British jazz musicians decided not to look towards America for inspiration any more. The daring baritone saxophonist **John Surman** was the one who proclaimed this new attitude in his celebrated album *Surman On the Mount*. Another was **Evan Parker**, whose saxophone playing was so much his own thing that it didn't even sound like saxophone playing.

This led the clarinettist **Sandy Brown**, who died of architecture and Scotch at the age of 46, to exclaim: 'I'll defend to the last his right to play like that, but I reserve my right not to listen to him' – the safest attitude for all but the most reckless bluffer to adopt when confronted with extremes of Own Thingism.

FAMOUS NAMES

You can tell that jazz is now of great historical importance because, as in classical music, most of the people that are well-known are dead. In spite of this, most of the names in the following brief 'Who's Who' still mean a lot to the rabid jazz-fan, and it is wise to know a little about each of them.

The important thing, however, is that this is a list and lists create more interest than almost anything in jazz. Particularly if they are lists of the one hundred top tuba players or something like that. It is the vital matter of who has been left out and who has been so thoughtlessly included.

These thumbnail sketches include most of the people you ought to know something about. There are those who will undoubtedly ask where are **Casper Reardon**, **Silas Cluke** and **Horsecollar Draper**. We feel the same.

Armstrong, Louis (c.1900-71)
Although without question one of the great names of jazz and one of its finest musicians, he caused quite a lot of embarrassment in his time. His trumpet playing remained superb but it was where it was heard that tended to upset a lot of people. So did his garbage disposal machine-type voice. Purists always considered he had lost credence after the early small groups of the 1920s.

After that he organised his decline by playing with large dance bands, appearing in films with people like Danny Kaye and Frank Sinatra, recording *Hello Dolly* and other best-selling items and fronting an All-Star group that seemed to have forgotten what it was that somebody thought they heard Buddy Bolden say. But he kept to his principles and always ate his diet before a good meal. A good favourite choice of an Armstrong recording would be *I'm a ding dong daddy* (1930) in which he done forgot his words.

Basie, William 'Count' (1904-84)
Apart from leading one of the most infectiously swinging bands of all time, Count Basie is celebrated for two things. One was his piano style which got (and more effective) as he grew older, so that during the last 46 years of his life he played fewer notes (but more music) than many pianists play in an evening. Hence the slogan: 'The less he played, the more he conveyed.' It was said that 'he even made the spaces in between the notes count' – which, of course, is where his nickname really came from.

Bechet, Sidney (1897-1969)
Developed an incredibly forceful style on the soprano-saxophone so that discographers never have any doubt that he is around. Try something like *Nobody knows the way I feel this mornin'* (1940) and you'll see why.

Beiderbecke, Bix (1903-31)
One of the great legends of jazz. A dedicated alcoholic who died young and spent his brief working career playing in big bands led by maestros like Jean Goldkette, Frankie Trumbauer and Paul Whiteman. In spite of this, his bell-like, singing, whisky-flavoured tone shone through many a musical morass like a good deed in a naughty world You can't go wrong with *I'm comin, Virginia* or *Singin' the blues*, both recorded, in spite of Trumbauer, in 1927. As long as you don't mind waiting for the Bix bits.

Bolden, Charles 'Buddy' (1877-1931)
Shadowy historic character long known as the Demon
Barber of Bourbon Street and a fearless gossip colum-
nist, partly on the strength of the garbled memories
of such people as Bunk Johnson. Scholastic researchers
have since destroyed these legends. What is left is the
vague possibility that he helped to establish many of
the jazz conventions, played the cornet the wrong way
round (see famous Bolden photo) and, when he blew
it, could be heard anything from four to fourteen miles
away depending on what he had been drinking. The
only surviving Bolden recording is in the possession
of the authors of this book so it is no good you making
any claims in that direction.

Carter, Benny (b. 1907)
Not only one of the greatest arrangers of jazz after
Fate Marable (he organised all sessions by black
jazzmen in the 1930s except those by name bands like
Ellington's) but also one of its most versatile musicians; playing and recording on alto-saxophone, tenor-
saxophone, clarinet, trumpet and trombone – though
not (like Roland Kirk) all at the same time. Arranged
for Henry Hall and may be heard singing on *The Teddy
Bear's Picnic*.

Coleman, Ornette (b.1930)
Just as the cinema organ world was full of Reginalds,
so is jazz heavily populated by Colemen: Coleman
Hawkins, **Bill** Coleman, **George** Coleman, **Earl**
Coleman, **Leslie** Coleman McCann (who pretends he
isn't by calling himself Les McCann), **Oliver** Coleman,
Davie Coleman, **Dorlan** Coleman, **Cy** Coleman –
not to mention **Cozy** and **Nat** 'King' Cole, man. But
the most controversial Coleman is Ornette, so-called

38

because the critics realised as soon as they heard him that they would be poking their typewriters into an ornette's nest of artistic discomfiture. Having been once bitten by Charlie Parker 16 years earlier they were now twice as shy. Ornette played a plastic alto; he blew little bursts of often quite catchy melody; you couldn't count the bars but his drummers usually went tish-ti-tish like in the old days.

Traditionalist listeners, recognizing a fellow primitive, frequently took to him right away. Now the term avant-garde has fallen out of favour, Ornette (which is the bit you use) is almost an establishment figure; currently using an orthodox metal saxophone – though he calls what he plays on it 'harmolodic' music and nobody knows what that means. He still plays violin occasionally and nobody knows what that means either.

Coltrane, John (1926-67)
Responsible for the fact that most jazz saxophone playing since the sixties has had a granite-like hardness. A fifties junkie (it is safe to assume that everybody was supported by something in the 50s, even if it was only by Dr. J. Collis Browne's mixture), musical dedication and iron discipline enabled him to kick the habit in 1967. Then he discovered God and the harp.

At the same time he created a style of playing called Sheets of Sound. It was coined to describe Coltrane's wish to exhaust the possibilities of every tune he tackled by not only playing the relevant notes but every note of every related scale, more or less all at once. It needed a clever person to do it, and another to invent such a nicely ambiguous name. Use it whenever you can and never forget to refer to Coltrane as 'Trane'.

Condon, Eddie (1905-73)
The Fate Marable of New York. He seems to have
arranged most of the Dixieland sessions in that city,
many of them for a high cover charge in his own Club.
His favourite recipe began 'take the juice of two
whiskies'. A disciple of **Silas Cluke**, his own banjo
and guitar playing has passed into justifiable neglect
but he was always there or thereabouts.

Davis, Miles (1926-91)
Miles Davis in his lifetime had to endure racial
prejudice, insult, misunderstanding, the effects of
acquiring and then kicking the heroin habit,
prolonged illness, great pain, immoderate adulation
and a lot of money. In their turn audiences, promoters,
some personal acquaintances and one or two fellow
musicians had to endure Miles Davis. The fact is that,
like many another genius, Miles (always call him
Miles by the way) was as cuddly as a cactus.

Any conversation about him starts from the
assumption that no matter what his musical sur-
roundings, his actual trumpet playing always remained
the same. Don't question this unless you're looking
for trouble. You might do yourself a bit of good by
casually pointing out that Miles was the only jazz
musician whose audiences got younger as he got older.
He contrived this very cunningly by playing adult jazz
at 19, jazz-rock at 39 and straight rock at 59.

In the 1950s he became notorious for turning his
back on the audience. By the mid-80s he had developed a method of walking slowly backwards all over
the stage bent nearly double, paying out little slivers
of melody as he went. Both habits were probably
completely without significance, but you mustn't let
that deter you from profound speculation.

Ellington, 'Duke' (1899-1974)

Renowned nobleman of jazz who actually managed to keep a band going from the early 1920s to his death. He made his reputation with 'jungle' noises played for the well lined clientele of the Cotton Club. He reached a peak of creativity in the 1940s then spent much of the subsequent years in repeating himself in a less effective way. His achievement was so great, however, that most people tend to forgive his frequent lapses. The Ellington sound was a saxophonist called **Johnny Hodges**.

Freeman, Lawrence 'Bud' (1906-91)

Someone once said to Bud: 'You look like a doctor but you play like a murderer.' It is certainly true that he dressed in a dapper fashion (he once did a one-off modelling job on the strength of it) and played in a huffing and puffing manner like a big bad wolf.

His style on tenor-saxophone was entirely his own creation, with a vibrato like washing flapping in the breeze. He was that rarity, a Chicago jazzman actually born in Chicago. The most important thing to seize on is whether or not he was an influence on **Lester Young**. You can take either view for it is difficult to tell.

Gillespie, 'Dizzy' (b.1917)

Distinctive trumpeter co-founder of the Minton school, hailed along with Parker and others as a god of be-boppery. Added to his uniqueness by playing on a special trumpet with its bell permanently pointed toward the heavens. Having long overstrained his cheek muscles he always looks to be on the point of having a facial explosion. He is thus able to blow as many as thirty-six fairly rapid notes with one puff.

41

Goodman, Benny (1909-86)
Crowned King of Swing in 1935 at a ceremony attended
only by his manager, his agent, his bank-manager
and Pee Wee Russell. The idea worked well and
subsequently drew immense besotted crowds to all
Goodman concerts. The only people who were peeved
about it were Paul Whiteman (who had not so long
before been crowned King of Jazz and felt he ought to
have been consulted) and one or two other bandleaders
who wished they had thought of the idea first.

Hampton, Lionel (b.1909)
Multi-instrumental genius who played the piano like
a vibraphone, the vibraphone like a piano, the drums
like mad and everything very loud and fast.

Hawkins, Coleman (1901-69)
After Louis Armstrong had been lord of the roost for
several years with everyone trying to copy him; Coleman
Hawkins came along with the 'new-fangled' saxophone (recently invented in 1846) and showed the jazz
world the next way of doing things; chiefly by playing
Body and soul with feeling. Always referred to as 'Bean'
because of his broad tone.

Henderson, Fletcher (1897-1952)
Led a big mushy sounding band at the Roseland
Ballroom in New York for many years. It occasionally
sounded distinguished because of the likes of Louis
Armstrong, Joe Smith or Coleman Hawkins in the
ranks. A thoughtful kind of man, he was known as
'Deep' Henderson. Having put the Swing Era in
motion, he became staff arranger for Benny Goodman
and squandered so many smackers his nickname was
changed to 'Smack'.

Herman, 'Woody' (1913-87)
Clarinet-playing bandleader who rather rudely referred
to his musicians as The Herd. The First Herd was
succeeded by the Second and the Second by the Third.
By the end he had got up to about Sixteen but had
long since given up numbering them. His original
band, prior to all this, were a friendly Dixielandish lot
and did well in 1939 out of a number called the
Woodchoppers Ball. This did a lot for woodchoppers in
the USA; and for a while it was taken over by the fur-
trappers union but the *Fur-trappers Ball* never seemed
quite the same. 'It was a great number', said Mr
Herman, 'the first thousand times we played it.'

Hines, Earl (1903-83)
Distinguished a) because he was a real Earl and didn't
pinch his title like all those phoney Kings, Dukes and
Counts; and b) because he always contrived to keep
his playing fresh and original using up to 57 different
varieties of approach.

Holiday, Billie (1915-59)
The Judy Garland of jazz.

Jackson, Mahalia (1911-72)
One of the first of the well-known holy red hot mommas,
she refused to be drawn into the commercial world of
jazz and blues, convinced that it was better to get rich
by promoting the gospel.

Johnson, Bunk (1889-1949)
Veteran New Orleans trumpeter who tried to adjust
the history of jazz by altering his birthdate so that it
fitted in with his own claims. Much of what he said was
believed by early historians and people have been trying

to straighten things out ever since. Rediscovered in a toothless condition in 1939 (working, so it is said, as a whistler in a fairground, whatever that is and however one manages to do it without teeth) he made some recordings in 1942 with other New Orleans veterans that perpetuated even more legends about how rough and out-of-tune genuine New Orleans jazz had been.

Johnson, James P. (1894-1955)
Brilliant pianist of the Harlem school who played with great delicacy and finesse in spite of looking like a boxing promoter – complete with cigar.

Kenton, Stan (1912-79)
Bandleader who made the fundamental mistake of telling everybody what he thought he was doing, instead of waiting for them to tell *him*. So when, in the late 40s, he announced that the enormous noise his band was making was progressive jazz, the only people who really believed him were those who didn't like jazz anyway.

He would call his records (and sometimes his concerts) *Artistry in This and That* and *Innovations in the Other*; a practice which particularly annoyed the critics because words like 'artistry' and 'innovation' belonged exclusively to them and weren't supposed to be used by anyone else. Thus 'progressive' became something of a dirty word; and we suggest you never employ it yourself unless you say it in quotes, as it were. If you do hear it used it will almost certainly be in connection with that period when S. Kenton, noting that the dancing audience was getting smaller and smaller, made his band bigger and bigger and went on a progress – not round the dancehalls but the theatres, turning jazz into a concert music.

La Rocca, Nick (1889-1961)
Leading light of the **Original Dixieland Jazz Band**,
who made the first jazz records, supplying a brash
cornet lead and writing a number of things for it that
frequently turned out to have been by someone else,
e.g. *Tiger rag*. The revival of the ODJB in 1936 was a
great relief to many: it proved it had only sounded so
odd in 1919 because of the primitive recording.

McKenzie, William 'Red' (1907-48)
The only exponent of the paper-and-comb in jazz to
become a household name. Led a group called the
Mound City Blue Blowers as kazooist and singer,
but is mainly remembered with gratitude as one who
found jobs for the boys in the Depression years.

Mezzrow, Milton 'Mezz' (1899-1972)
Variously remembered as:
a) co-author of a book of astonishing frankness and
   raciness called *Really the Blues,*
b) such a successful purveyor of narcotics that the
   marijuana cigarette was nicknamed a 'mezz' in his
   honour;
c) a laid-back clarinettist on some historical sessions
   organised by Hugues Panassié;
d) having been described by Mr. Hentoff as 'the Baron
   Munchausen of jazz', and
e) volunteering to be black and blue.

Mulligan, Gerry (b.1927)
When Gerry Mulligan first came on the scene at the
end of the 1940s, the huge piece of plumbing he
played was still a 'miscellaneous instrument' according
to the jazz popularity polls of the day. With one mighty
puff he gained for the baritone-saxophone recognition

as an instrument in its own right. He had sufficient
lung power also to blow the piano out of his way, and
his greatest fame followed the foundation in 1952 of
the piano-less **Gerry Mulligan Quartet**. Pianists
sulked and contemplated union action, but even they
had to admit that it made a wonderful noise – cool
but not cold.

By 1955, when commercial television started up in
Britain, the effect had become so popular that, for a
few years, the music to every other TV ad seemed to
be by the GMQ. He has a nickname, Geru', but use of
it could suggest over zealous bluffing. Watch for its
incautious use by others and chalk it up against them.

Nichols, Ernest Loring 'Red' (1905-65)

Fortunate in having red hair so that he didn't have to
be referred to either as Ernest or Loring – two names
entirely unsuitable for jazz purposes – he made his
name leading a jerky New York Dixieland band of
from 6 to 10 players which he subtly called the **Five
Pennies** (nickel = penny; get it). Gained even more
renown after having a romanticised film based on his
life in which he was played by Danny Kaye.

Parker, Charlie (1920-56)

Charlie 'Yardbird' Parker was the first jazz musician
to be elected to the Wall of Fame. Within hours of his
breathing his last, the legend 'BIRD LIVES!' had been
daubed on the walls of the New York subway.
Although he died, as one commentator said, 'of everything', he was now officially immortal.

After Louis Armstrong, he is, in fact, the most
immortal jazz person you will have to bluff about. He
didn't quite start modern jazz single-handed because
there were others around at the time, like **John Birks**,

46

'Dizzy' Gillespie and Thelonious Monk, who were involved as well. But it's safe to say (and you should) that if Monk had been a Birk and if Gillespie had been a monk, Parker would have created rebop, bebop, and just plain bop, all the same. He did this by playing, on alto-saxophone, well-known pop tunes so fast and so brilliantly that no-one could recognise them. He also gave them new titles, which confused everyone still further (it will be useful for you to remember that *Cherokee* by Ray Noble became *Koko* by Charlie Parker; Duke Ellington wrote an entirely different *Koko*, which begins to look like a conspiracy).

Charlie Parker had a New York club named after him, Birdland, which became so full even he couldn't get in.

Pianists: **Oscar Peterson** (b.1925), **John Lewis** (b.1920), **Erroll Garner** (1921-77) and **Dave Brubeck** (b.1920)

That you find yourself bluffing about jazz at all could well be because of one or more of these four pianists – give or take a Waller or two. What they had in common was the ability, especially in the 1950s and 60s, to persuade an immense audience that God would not smite them with a plague of boils if they went to a jazz concert. By becoming very popular and earning more than a bare living, these Big Four offended many jazz purists who reached for their most potent insult – 'commercial'. It might be as well for you to ascertain the attitude of your co-bluffers before you take a definite stance on these artists.

A useful point to remember about **Oscar Peterson** ('Oscar' to you) is that he was born and still lives in

Canada. He is physically very large and only the huge Bösendorfer piano, with its extra bottom notes, can accommodate him. He usually works with a trio and gives his drummers a hard time. For emergency use, keep up your sleeve the knowledge that his singing voice is uncannily like Nat 'King' Cole's – another 'commercial'.

John Lewis is in an ambivalent position. He played, in the early days, with Charlie Parker, which is as near as you can get in the jazz world to getting a sainthood. On the other hand he dreamed up the idea of the **Modern Jazz Quartet**, dressed as if for a funeral, to play beautifully swinging music which people could understand and made a large amount of money. You can tell what a questionable notion it was from the way it only managed to last, with a hiatus in the 70s, from 1952 to the present day.

All pianists grunt as they play, but **Erroll Garner** played as he grunted – and louder than anyone else had cared to. Nobody really minded because he swung like the clappers, in spite of the way his left hand seemed to be loitering with intent. Audiences loved him for his personality was enormous even though Garner himself (for some reason his surname is a permissible one) was so short that he had to take a copy of the Manhattan telephone directory round with him to sit on while he played.

Dave Brubeck is another pianist/leader who attracted listeners to jazz in droves, though it is true to say that for every punter (a useful word) who came to tap a foot to Brubeck's Gothic keyboard work, there were two who stayed to nod their heads to the graceful alto-saxophone of **Paul Desmond**. If you get the chance, make it plain that you know it was Paul Desmond who wrote *Take Five*, not Brubeck.

Russell, Charles Ellsworth 'Pee Wee' (1906-69)

With a name like Ellsworth to obscure, even being called 'Pee Wee' could be an improvement. A face like an English aristocrat who has gone astray and become a bookie; and a clarinet tone that sounded like it smoked too much; Mr. Russell was, not surprisingly, one of the great individualists of jazz and everything he played was rather unexpected; even though he spent most of his playing career in somewhat bland company. A true jazz eccentric.

Spanier, Francis 'Muggsy' (1906-1967)

His slightly squashed but homely features suggested, wrongly as he would explain, why he was called 'Muggsy'. Played a warm, talkative plunger-muted cornet style that came to true fame when a Dixieland group called the **Ragtimers** just happened to do everything in the right way at the right time in 1939. Dedicated one of his best numbers to the Touro hospital in New Orleans where he was successfully cured of the jazzman's disease.

Tatum, Art (1909-1956)

One-eyed, twelve-fingered Los Angeles pianist who was highly rated in the 40s as the player who could score the most runs per minute. After Tatum all jazz pianists had to have alcohol free instruments provided so that they could have a shot at matching his technique.

Teagarden, Jack (1905-1964)

Highly rated trombonist who played with a Texan drawl and sang as if he had a perpetual hangover. The white man's answer to Louis Armstrong, he frequently duetted with the maestro in *Ol' rockin' chair's got me* and similar front-porch songs.

Waller, Thomas 'Fats' (1904-1943)
Jovially satirical pianist, organist and singer. Fighting weight around 24 stone. Composer of *Ain't misbehavin'* and *Honeysuckle rose* and a champion imbiber of liquor; he passed away at a sadly early age in a train that was running late between Los Angeles and New York.

Young, Lester (1909-1959)
Celebrated as the coolest of the hot tenors and for his pork pie hats which he even wore in bed. The last of the saxophonists to please the Panassiés because he swung and played in a melodic manner; and the first to please the modernists because he paved the way to Parkerism. Did much of his best work in the Basie band filling in the wide open spaces between the notes the Count played. He was dubbed 'Pres' by Billie Holiday and the bluffer should always do likewise.

Zwerin, Mike (b.1930)
Trombonist famous for always being the last entry in jazz reference books.

HOW TO TALK JAZZ

As with anything that has pretensions to being an art form, the enjoyment of the beholder stems more from talking about jazz than actually listening to it. It even rivals the pleasures of collecting it.

Obviously a sense of being 'in touch' is eminently desirable if your bluff is to be effective. It is certainly not necessary to adopt all the involved linguistic armoury of the jazz world – the conversational address of 'man', the reference to all third parties as 'cats', general appreciation as digging, and so on. This sort of thing, done without the conviction that comes so naturally to an inhabitant of Harlem, can be disastrous when tackled in the feeble manner of any Briton trying to emulate an American accent, or vice versa. Better to stick with more moderate equivalents of the above, such as 'my dear chap', 'guys' and 'being knocked out by', respectively.

The accolade 'really swinging' says all that need be said. It reaches way beyond mere physical movement. It means that everything is well and truly right. Indeed it can be applied to many things that are not swinging at all in the 1930s sense. Other expressions to indicate your approval are 'earthy' and 'funky' – both suggesting a commitment to the spirit of jazz.

It is a good thing to refer to all jazz instruments as 'horns', even pianos, drums and things. Likewise all instruments in jazz (whether of the wind variety or not) are 'blown' and not played. One does not refer to performances or concerts but rather to 'gigs' or sessions, the latter not merely confined to recordings.

Another important matter is the contradictory epithet which is used in authentic jazz circles. The most common occurrence is in the use of the word 'bad' which is taken to mean 'superb'. Thus, if you slip into saying something like "I thought his timing was bad" you will inadvertently have been praise-heaping.

Ultimately the vocabulary is of less importance than your general attitude. For instance, you must have a sense of period. Take Duke Ellington as a sample subject. Refer to him as 'Duke' or 'The Duke'. You would be expected to know what was implied by succinct reference to his 20s style (jungle noises over a bouncing tuba and banjo background); his 30s style (jungle noises over a string bass and guitar background with optional timpani); the 40s – big band (at least 12 men) stuff coloured by the genius of a short-lived bass player called **Blanton**; the 50s – rather more pretentious stuff with modernistic chords thrown in by an assistant pianist called **Strayhorn**; the 60s – general decline.

You must understand that the demanding nature of jazz means that all jazzmen decline very quickly. After a brief period of being underrated they find their distinctive tone, make the recordings by which they will always be known in their twenties, get ambitious in their thirties and in their forties start on the road to oblivion.

As a large percentage of jazzmen tend to leave this world (the result of occupational or liquid excesses) at quite an early age, forty is considered a very mature vintage. It is difficult to think of many prominent jazzmen who have not declined. Some have simply remained permanently pickled, but generally most of them signal their getting out of touch by trying to do what they once did naturally and well in what they themselves consider to be a mature manner but which, to the discerning bluffer, simply shows a lack of spontaneity and even integrity. Very few jazzmen mature well.

One manifestation of loss of integrity is the big band wish. Jazzmen who made a respectable reputation by playing with as few as two other people (or in cases of extreme hardship one other, or by themselves), having moved to success with groups varying from five to seven players, then get the urge to front (i.e. to stand in front of, for publicity shots) a big band.

Even this can be forgiven if the results remain funky enough, but many jazzmen, even quite modern ones, often get illusions of grandeur at this point and signal their complete decline by the lavish employment of a string section. It is safe to say that all string sections have been disastrous in jazz.

There are many approaches to adopt, most of them based on various critical factions. A lot of early jazz talk came from a book called *Jazzman* which adopted a friendly sort of tone, e.g:

'He had a vibrato that was in keeping with his sweeping crescendos, and just a touch of blue quality. While he played he seemed oblivious of the smoke-filled room and of the dancers. He sat hunched forward, his clarinet pointed towards the floor'; and,

'When the band "went crazy" after the funeral, the kids cut up with their primitive version of the "Susie Q" and danced the "shudders".'

Jazz enthusiasts still lap up that kind of thing.

Jazzmen, published in 1939, clearly belongs to the romantic age of jazz literature, indeed to the romantic age of jazz itself when it was important to build up colour and background rather than go into detailed discussions of the music. By the 1950s an altogether different brand of critic was in command, e.g:

'The theoretician might claim that the blues scale is none other than that of the mode of D, designated by some historians as the Dorian. Actually the blues scale has quite a different nature and is to be distinguished from the Greek mode by the variability of its blue notes. The third and seventh degrees are lowered or not depending on how open or how disguised an allusion to the major scale is desired. Frequently, blue notes and unaltered examples of the same degree occur within a single phrase. Sometimes the two are superimposed, and in such cases the blue note's being a kind of suspended appoggiatura is emphasized.'

Of course, in the early days, no one guessed that the player hunched forward with his clarinet pointed toward the floor was actually suffering from a suspended appoggiatura. Many died of similar things before this was found out; whereas today they could be saved.

Discography

There are a number of jazz enthusiasts who never go near any live jazz. They listen to it entirely on records. This has inevitably led them into the false belief that this is where jazz exists. When they blithely burble about Armstrong's 1934 period they are thinking entirely about the Armstrong sounds they happen to have on disc. This tends to make jazz musicians mad. Most were toiling away somewhere every night and the few hours they spent in the recording studio were, to them, of minor significance; probably not even representing what they considered their best work.

It is partly the fault of jazz itself. Not being available in the shape of a score, the only evidence we can depend on is what the gramophone record has preserved for posterity. Most jazz could not be written down and disappears for ever the moment it is played – or would if it were not for the occasional recording engineer being around at the time. As most jazz talk is about jazz on record, the bluffer had better be well briefed in this department.

The true jazz collector (i.e record collector) was, at one time, only interested in 78s. It was considered not to be the real thing unless it sounded as if it was being played several streets away with a rusty nail.

As not many will enjoy the opportunity to own an original Gennett, Paramount or Okeh (early jazz record labels – the possession of which would be the equivalent of having a Shakespeare first folio) it has become all right to collect later re-issues on 78s (or even LPs) – so long as the original background noise is preserved. The principal pastime with old 78s was to identify who was on them, so the dimness of the sound was simply an additional challenge. It was a lot more fun in the early days when the experts had not reached so many conclusions.

But there are still plenty of unsolved mysteries to promote enjoyable arguments. These generally revolve around who was playing, let us say, the cornet on the 1925 recording by the **Mississippi Ramblers**. It had boldly been assumed, notably by Delaunay, that this was a group led by the redoubtable King Oliver; but others doubted this as it was on the Autophone label and, at that time, Oliver was recording for Gennett. Should someone hazard a guess that it was **Jazzum Jenkins** you could pour scorn on this on account of the prominent use of the mute. Jenkins, as far as you know (which is not all that far really), never used a mute. A broken beer glass occasionally, but never a mute which it clearly is here; unless he was standing behind a pillar.

Delaunay lists six instruments – cornet, trombone, C-melody sax, piano, banjo and drums – but, unless our ears deceive us, there is almost certainly a second cornet there, sounding remarkably like **Eddie 'Splitnote' Rackstraw**. You will remember him on that unissued Morton session from the same year. Can it be denied that the 2-note phrase with which he backs the alto-sax solo (which we believe it to be in spite of what McCarthy, Rust and Delaunay say) is, as anyone can hear, almost identical (apart from the fact that it is two different notes) from the one he used there?

If it is Rackstraw then surely the first cornet must be **Lawson 'Tightlips' Evans** who regularly played with him in the 1920s. Mind you, that is only on the strength of what Bunk Johnson said, so it could be doubtful. Delaunay names the C-melody sax (sic) as **Bertrand Stillwater** and there would be little reason to doubt this, if it really was a C-melody, as he was active in Chicago at the time. But to say that **Ed Atkins** was on trombone seems to be just wild guess-work. And so it goes on.

The collector is particularly intrigued by alternative takes. As most early jazzmen on most early sessions were inclined to be playing under the influence of alcohol, or something, the takes were inclined to be many in number.

It is a well-known fact, even in today's highly professional recording circles, that having tried seven or eight alternative versions of a given piece the producer always decides that the first take was the best anyway; and this is generally the one issued. But occasionally someone misunderstands the producer's scrawl and types out Take 3 instead. This becomes an everlasting source of discographical interest.

In the expansive LP era it became the thing to re-issue all the alternative takes side by side so that the collector could hear what went wrong. You can now hear for yourself how things got progressively worse as the alcohol took effect and the trombonist's lips fell apart. Some scrupulous editors have dug around and put out every scrap of discarded tape, even those of but a few second's duration. It is an ineffable delight to the earnest collector to hear Charlie Parker bitterly complaining that he is having reed trouble.

The modern collector has to make do with CDs and has his jazz ruined for him by over-clear recordings which leave almost nothing in doubt, including the great tedium of endless solos inspired only by the commercial need to fill two sides of a record. Moreover, modern record producers spoil all the fun by giving, on the record sleeve, all the details of what went on. Sadly, it seems that discography might be becoming a bit of a lost art.

But two pieces of harmless discographical pleasure remain. One comes from the fact that though the durations of tracks are often printed on labels and/or record sleeves, they are always wrong – not by a minute or any explainable misprint, but by some arbitrary amount. When all other conversation has lapsed, you can always take out your stopwatch and run a book on who can guess the nearest correct answer.

The other is the habit indulged in by some compilers of re-issues, of splicing together solos from different takes of the same tune. The object of the game in this instance is to try to spot the joins in what purports to be one continuous performance. It's the musical equivalent of wig-spotting.

GLOSSARY

Big Band Jazz – Purist's term of abuse for: a) any
group containing more than seven players; b) any
group that has two or more saxophones in it.
Mainly an outsider's term. Musicians much in
favour of the whole idea refer to it as 'the bread'.
bread'. See also Swing.

Broonzy – Jazz man's name for an over-large
invoice.

Chocolate – Acceptably jocular term, much used in
show business. Various other terms have derived
from it; 'soft-centre' and 'hard-centre' styles; 'after-
eight' (a musician who can't play until he's had a
coffee); an 'aero' – a jazzman who has just had an
argument with Al Capone.

Commercial – Term of abuse for jazz that is likely to
appeal to the general public, a body of people much
despised by the jazz fraternity.

Corn – Term of abuse for jazz that is likely to appeal
to the general public, who are frequently referred
to by the jazz fraternity as cornflakes.

Creole – A term of respectability, implying some useful (especially French) inter-breeding and lighter
shades of black. Used as an elevating title by bands
such as Creole Jazz Band who were uniformly
dark.

Dixieland – A source of total confusion since
Dixieland, as a geographical term, means the

Southern States with banjos strumming and all that jazz; but as a generic term (because of the Original Dixieland Jazz Band) is generally applied to white groups playing in a frivolous style and wearing bowler hats.

Funky – Smelly. Has occasionally been linked with the word 'butt', meaning a bottom. Fortunately it has changed its meaning somewhat to imply earthiness, bluesness, gospelarity, Africanality, etc.

Gone – Term used, in the peculiarly boomerang manner of much jazz terminolgy, to imply a definite state of being here, and going places.

Growl – Noise made by an underpaid trombonist.

Hip – Erstwhile hep. The state of being in the know. Refer to a jazz club as a hip-bath, a jazz festival as a hip operation, and so on.

Hot – The most glowing tribute you can pay to traditional jazz. A mind-singeing way of playing. Known as warm when applied to mainstream jazz, and cool when applied to modern.

Humph – Verb meaning to blow hard in any profitable direction.

Jam – When everyone plays together with no clear idea of where they are going or even what they are playing. Chiefly amusing to those who are doing it but occasionally results, by chance, in something coherent and exciting.

Jive – In the past (1930s), a hectic type of dancing also known as jitterbugging in the pre-rock world. Now more usually applied to jazz talk. A telling phrase in any bluffer's vocabulary, said in tones of deep disbelief, is: "Don't give me that jive, mate!"

Mouldy Fig – The sort of person who likes or plays Trad.

Name Band – Friendly sort of outfit ready to do anything to please the public, the title deriving from the phrase: 'You name it, we'll play it'.

Rhythm – The element in jazz that either you 'got' or didn't. Most disliked by English vicars and old ladies in the early days as it tended to rattle the cakestands.

Riff – A phrase generally repeated ad nauseam by sections of a big band. Deriving from the *Riff song*, a chorus repeated ad nauseam in *The Desert Song*.

Rock, Rocking – Originally another rude word connected with sexual activity but latterly attached to jazz in the purely descriptive sense of a band that is really swinging, in the groove, or what-have-you. Much used by English dance bands of the thirties during their summer seasons, as in the Blackpool Rock, the Brighton Rock, and so on.

Scat – A method of getting over a temporary aberration concerning the words of any song.

Shimmy – A dance originated by Armond Piron's elder sister, Kate.

Shuffle – A dance step originated by reluctant males at endlessly boring dinner-dances.

Swing – Word used either as a verb to describe the sort of propulsive rhythm to which, in the words of an old song, 'the foot tappeth and the ale sloppeth'; or adjectively, as when Louis Armstrong in the 1930s talkie *Old Bones of the River* (later retitled for black audiences *Fate Cannot Harm Me*) ejaculated: 'You're really swingin' tha, Pops'; or as a noun to describe the sort of music played by jazz-oriented dance bands playing for an exclusively white audience in clubs and dance-halls. The word has caused much confusion and at times jazz has been referred to as 'swing music'. It is generally agreed now that swing is that which is played by Big Bands.

Trad – Double meaning of: a) a piece of music that can freely be used because nobody knows who wrote it and it costs nothing; b) jazz played by mouldy figs.

Wail, **Wailing** – Contrary to what one might think, a complimentary term for one who is playing with considerable savoir-faire and soul.

Whiteman – One who pays well for a musician's services and thus tempts him from the righteous path.

A Question of Jazz

By way of testing what you have gleaned from this book (however minuscule) we append a short questionnaire.

1. Explain (in not more than 700 words) why nobody ever seems to have gone down the river.

2. Why are the following world-renowned: a) Dudley Fosdick b) Horsecollar Draper c) Victor Houseman?

3. What was it they said about Dixie – and was it actually true?

4. Where did British jazz begin: a) Eel Pie Island b) Crayford Conservative Club c) The Old Red Barn?

5. What is the significance of the following in jazz, and how would you handle it: a) Rust b) Feather c) Godbolt?

6. Who took the photograph of Buddy Bolden? What with? Why did Bolden refuse to pay for it?

7. How high the moon?

8. What would you do with a goofus: a) play it b) cook it c) send it back to the maker?

9. How do you spell: a) Milenberg b) Featherstonaugh c) Bauduc?

10. What was it that: a) Sister Kate could do that you couldn't; b) you ain't gonna give nobody none of; c) was the way hotcha do it?

11. How far is it from: a) Natchez to Mobile b) Acheson to Peka c) here to Tipperary?

12. How would you cook: a) Patois b) mouldy figs c) a jelly roll?

THE AUTHORS

Peter Clayton was born in the Deep South of London well below the Fortnum-Mason Line. After a career as a porridge taster and local librarian, he wandered into an anonymous-looking building in Brixton and found himself working for a record company. After several years effort to get out, he managed to escape by a short wavelength and found he was working as a broadcaster.

By devious means, such as letting it all happen, he gradually took over several key programmes, sometimes heavily disguised, and joined the ranks of the BBC's immovables, gracing the air with his wit and wisdom until his death in 1991.

Peter Gammond was born on the far North-West frontier in a Depression. After passing through Oxford, leaving a trail of half-finished poems and an old trombone, he ended up in the same disused nail factory in Brixton that Peter Clayton was soon to enter. As Wordsworth wrote (in another context):

> The ways were long and narrow,
> The twain were short and wide;
> It really was inevitable
> Their courses should collide.'

They worked together on various musico-literary projects, finding a perfect form of collaboration by both working on the same bits, then discarding the one with the least number of ambiguities. Their joint efforts included: *Fourteen Miles on a Clear Night* (later retitled *22.53 Kilometres in a High Pressure Zone*) and *The Jazz Man's A-Z of Guinness*.

THE BLUFFER'S GUIDES

Available at £1.99 and (new titles* £2.50) each:

Accountancy	Marketing
Advertising	Maths
Antiques	Modern Art
Archaeology	Motoring
Astrology & Fortune Telling	Music
Ballet	The Occult
Bird Watching	Opera
Bluffing	Paris
British Class	Philosophy
Champagne*	Photography
The Classics	P.R.
Computers	Public Speaking
Consultancy	Publishing
Cricket	Racing
The European Community	Secretaries
Espionage	Seduction
Finance	Sex
The Flight Deck	Small Business*
Golf	Teaching
The Green Bluffer's Guide	Theatre
Japan	University
Jazz	Weather Forecasting
Journalism	Whisky
Literature	Wine
Management	World Affairs

All these books are available at your local bookshop or newsagent, or can be ordered direct from the publisher. Prices and availability subject to change without notice. Just tick the titles you require and send a cheque or postal order (allowing in the UK for postage and packing 28p for one book and 12p for each additional book ordered) to:

Ravette Books Limited, 3 Glenside Estate, Star Road, Partridge Green, Horsham, West Sussex RH13 8RA.